Purposeful Living:
A Young Adult's Guide to Discovery

Purposeful Living:
A Young Adult's Guide to Discovery

Rhonda D. Gehle, M.A., M.S.

Corridor 314, LLC
2018

Copyright © 2018 by Rhonda D. Gehle

All rights reserved. This book or any portion thereof may not be reproduced or used in any manner whatsoever without the express written permission of the publisher except for the use of brief quotations in a book review or scholarly journal.

First Printing: 2018

ISBN 978-0-692-12442-0

Corridor 314, LLC

9955 E. Greenway St.

Mesa, AZ 85207

www.corridor314.com

Cover photo ©2011. Tim Gehle. All Rights Reserved. Used by permission.

Dedication

Briana, Brittany, and Katie: Thanks so much for walking through this with me and for your insightful feedback and suggestions. Blessings to you as you continue on your journey!

Family and close loved ones: You all know who you are who have contributed to my upbringing and done so with such love and grace that all I want to do is share that with others in return! My humble words of gratitude do not come close to expressing how thankful I am!

Tim: Your love and encouragement through this process mean more than I can even begin to articulate here. Thanks for believing in me and spurring me on to reach further and achieve more! Love you tons!!

Contents

Foreword 1
Program Introduction and Expectations 5
Chapter 1: Foundation 9
Chapter 2: Identity 17
Chapter 3: Strengths and Abilities 33
Chapter 4: Personality 39
Chapter 5: Passions and Values 47
Chapter 6: Experience 59
Chapter 7: Calling 67
Chapter 8: Life Purpose/Mission 75
Chapter 9: Conclusion 85
References 89

Foreword

Let's face it, understanding your purpose in life can be daunting and nebulous, and the pressures felt from society do not make it any easier. Some folks deal with this question long past their formative years and never really feel like they have settled into life pursuits that fit them well, that are somehow significant, that line up with their own strengths and values, and that they truly enjoy. Having dealt with this question in my own life as well as talked with many high school and college students about their college, career, and life plans, I think there is merit to taking a closer look at this topic. There are so many contributing factors that play into this and some of them can be very confusing. Family, culture, faith, talents, dreams, and even self-concept all may have a voice. If you find yourself confronted with this challenging and often puzzling life issue, please be assured that you are not alone!

I hope that this book will provide a resource for older teens and young adults, to help them think about their purpose in life, career plans, and life goals through a Christian worldview, with godly values as a foundation. Stanley (2008) says: "God has a purpose in mind for your life, and when you operate within its guidelines, you will excel far beyond anything you could imagine" (p. 29). If you find yourself facing these challenging issues and decisions, the goal for this journey is for you to better understand yourself, what you love to do, and how God is guiding your life. In short, this will prescribe for you some very valuable steps of self-discovery, help you further understand how God has created you and given you a unique and specific reason for being, and enable you to articulate a life purpose statement - a life mission - that will encompass who you are and what your life is about. It is an assignment in alignment; learning more about who you are so you can better align your life and decisions with God's bigger plan. My desire is that this will be useful as a tool for stimulating thoughtful discussions, guiding thought processes, providing encouragement and hope; and that it will be the basis for practical and wise decisions that will benefit each reader on the journey.

This guide is written for use in an ideal setting of a small group of 6 to 8 young adults. Input from others, accountability, and camaraderie will be very beneficial in this process. If you are not able to be part of a group, you can accomplish this study on your own if you are well-disciplined and focused. It would be helpful, though, if you could at least talk through your ideas and questions with a trusted friend or family member. This will help solidify your thoughts and impressions, and gaining another person's perspective will prove valuable. In addition, the study could be adjusted quite easily and used in a classroom setting with many opportunities for discussions and interactions among the members.

Program Introduction and Expectations

There seem to be many conversations taking place these days about intentional, purposeful living; about knowing what you're about and how to live that out. Some people go in search of a cause to support, others look for a reason for every circumstance in life to try to make meaning of it. Let's be honest that there are many things in life we will never fully understand on this side of heaven, but at the same time, let's embrace the idea that God made us to be actively and intentionally involved in furthering His Kingdom. The best way to do that is with focus, purpose, and passion!

Most successful companies and ministries invest time and effort into examining themselves and their goals in order to articulate a set of values, a mission, and even a vision statement. This means that they will look at their identity as a group, understand what they do well and what areas need work, identify their resources and how effectively they are being utilized, and make sure that what they are doing on a daily basis contributes to their main goals. Then they garner support from members so that everyone can work together in order to embrace the values, intentionally pursue the mission, and highlight the vision in as many ways as they can. This structure and definitions are then guides for daily decisions, how to use funds wisely, where to focus efforts, etc. This is the responsible way for a company or ministry to use the resources it has been given in order to accomplish their goals and be viable in their market or environment.

God made us to be actively and intentionally involved in furthering His Kingdom!

So, when thinking about how we can engage in intentional and purposeful living, there are many similar concepts we can use in order to do this type of analysis and planning in our own lives. The goal for this study is to provide a learning resource for late teens and young adults (emerging adults) to help with the processes of thinking about who you are and what your unique purpose and direction in life will be, to lay a foundation for a future filled with wise decisions that align with God's design, purposes, and calling, to begin discovering and defining personal passions and guiding values. As you start to consider decisions that are related to your future, this will be a tool that will guide those thought processes and help you move forward with focused intentions and sound rationales in place. All of these concepts are grounded in Scripture with the ultimate goal of furthering God's Kingdom and His eternal purposes.

This study will take you through some very practical exercises that will help you with who you are, what your strengths might be, how you should see yourself based on God's perspective, what kind of personality you have, articulation of values and worldview, how your past experiences have influenced your outlook, and where your passions lie. In a group setting, we will work with a variety of types of discovery activities and tools, discuss what we are noticing, and encourage one another in the process. If you are reading this book and working on these exercises alone, it would be very helpful for you to do a lot of journaling so you can capture your thoughts and ideas, and it would also increase the effectiveness of the program for you to be able to share these things with a trusted friend or family member. By doing these things, you will help solidify what you are learning and you will also have some input and feedback from another person that can provide further clarity. If you are not someone who enjoys writing or journaling, make sure to find a way to keep some notes for yourself, but then also to process your thoughts in a way that is comfortable for you - perhaps through verbal or artistic expression. There will be time allotted to begin to examine what you feel God has called you to do and what you believe is His purpose for you in the world. As a culminating application, you will examine what you have learned about yourself and use those observations and the guidance of the Holy Spirit to write a personal statement of life purpose/mission.

If you are working within a group, you will need to take some time before launching into the program to set some ground rules, expectations regarding commitment and meeting times, and boundaries for how your sharing will occur. Those specifics will be decided by each group and its leader. Remember that in a group it is important to be truly willing to hear others and be respectful of their contributions.

Chapter 1: Foundation

People have an innate need for God. Robert Roberts (2007) explains that this need can be defined as a need to feel secure – a sense of being able to trust someone or something completely and absolutely; to be loved – to know full acceptance and feel truly valued; and to have meaning – a sense of higher purpose and direction in life. Philosophers and psychologists have struggled for a long time to understand and put into words these internal cravings of the human soul and they have often ended up trying to fit God into their human conceptualizations. But the reality of it is that as humans we seek to fill those needs. Many pursue things that the world around us says will fulfill us: career success, status, material goods, money, fun, beauty, etc. But all too soon pursuing these things can begin to take over and become the full focus of our energies, the thing that dominates our thinking and decisions. Essentially, they become the gods of our life because those needs are what we serve, and yet we still feel unfulfilled and unsatisfied. It is no mistake that God's first two "commandments" or instructions of the covenant are strong statements to remind His children that He is the LORD God and that we should have no other gods before Him (Exodus 20). Knowing God and understanding His character, and having a personal and growing relationship with Him allows us to see that He is completely and utterly trustworthy (fulfills our need for security), He loves us with an unconditional love that is far beyond any level of human love (fulfills our need for love and acceptance), and He provides a sense of higher meaning and purpose to life here on earth as well as for eternity (fulfills our need for meaning). God alone is God. Getting this priority right in life is foundational and will save us a lot of searching after other things that do not satisfy us but rather end up leading us down a lot of unfulfilling and even destructive paths. Even so, we are only able to know God partially while we are here on earth, but as our relationship with Him deepens, it reaches further into our deepest longings and provides such sweet filling of that "God-shaped hole."

God alone is God.

The type of inner peace we can have as we grow in that relationship comes from relinquishing our control and allowing God to truly be God in our lives. Many Christians still live life thinking that their lives are their own and essentially self is at the center of their beliefs and decisions. But this is just a way of saying to God that we don't trust Him to be in charge and that we're not ready to be fully obedient. Jesus taught that we should deny ourselves, turn aside from our own desires, interests, rights, and self-centeredness, and follow Him (Matt. 16:24). In order to be true Christ followers, we must stop trusting in ourselves, fully believe that God is in absolute control and will accomplish His plans, and trust completely that He will provide for all our needs. This involves a daily choice to submit to Him, set aside our own agendas and worries, and walk in humble obedience before Him. Proverbs 3:5-6 sums this up so well. The New International Version says it like this: "Trust in the LORD with all your heart and lean not on your own understanding; in all your ways submit to Him and He will make your paths straight. Do not be wise in your own eyes; fear the LORD and shun evil." Another way of saying it is: "Trust GOD from the bottom of your heart; don't try to figure out everything on your own. Listen for GOD's voice in everything you do, everywhere you go; he's the one who will keep you on track. Don't assume that you know it all. Run to GOD! Run from evil!" (the Message).

We need to be willing to be different from the other sheep.

In his book "A Shepherd looks at Psalm 23," Phillip Keller (1970) makes some suggestions as to attitudes to adopt that can really help a Christian begin to walk in a more meaningful and submitted way – in a true Christ-follower relationship with Him. In his discussion about sheep (people) and the Shepherd (Jesus), he says, "Just as sheep will blindly, habitually, stupidly, follow one another along the same little trails until they become ruts that erode into gigantic gullies, so we humans cling to the same habits that we have seen ruin other lives" (p. 66). But if we want to avoid that type of unfulfilled path which often ends up leading to ruin, we need to be willing to be different from the other sheep and choose a way that leads to abundant life, wholeness, and holiness. Some attitudes include:

1) **Love God first, and others more than myself**. These are the principles Jesus taught in Matthew 22:37-39 and this echoed what was written in the Old Testament Law. This involves learning a lot of

selflessness in attitude and action. This kind of love is not a warm, fuzzy feeling; it is a choice, an act of the will.

2) **Be different, set apart.** Be willing to be counter-culture, not of this world, transformed rather than conformed (Rom. 12: 1-2). Please note that this mindset is not about being different in order to stand out and get attention. It is not about attracting others to myself, but rather it is about following Jesus' example and living in such a way as to draw others to Him. Jesus came and taught a whole new way of thinking and living which was radically different from what was accepted in His day. He taught about following the narrow path and being willing to forsake all others and all else to follow Him. The same is true today. We need to be ready to be different and take a stand.

3) **Lay aside my rights and preferences in favor of others** (Matt. 5: 1-12). This type of living means that I don't need to assert myself or make myself feel important in front of others. It may also be about a willingness to be a peacemaker and give what I believe to be rightly mine for the sake of others. In a world where those who stand up to exercise personal rights are heralded as heroes, Jesus calls me to deny myself and set aside my pride and self-importance.

4) **Strive daily to please God and let Him direct my path** (Prov. 3: 5-7). In doing this, I release my need to be in control or be the boss and practice fully submitting to His Lordship and leadership in my life. I do not need to promote myself or look for ways to move ahead; I do need to continually be willing to do what God asks of me and allow Him to manage and direct my life and all its parts.

5) **Accept life and its circumstances with gratitude and contentment.** This is contrasted with finding fault, complaining, asking why with an attitude of entitlement, and even adopting a victim mentality. It can be so freeing to set aside the negativity and embrace the positives in life and the Giver of the many gifts and blessings of life. Be thankful on a daily basis, live life with an attitude of gratitude, and truly trust that all of life is in God's hands and that His desire is for my good and His glory (Col. 2: 6-7).

6) **Be willing to set aside my will and ways to follow His will and ways.** Part of being a true follower of Christ is daily putting to death my own wants and wishes and cooperating fully with what He has for me (Luke 9:23). Being transformed means being changed from the inside out in order to align myself fully with God's will and walk obediently in His ways.

Discussion:

Consider how God fulfills our basic needs all the way to our complex needs because of our relationship with Him. Give an example of how you have seen this in your life.

What is the main theme you see in this chapter?

Assignment:

Review the foundational principles discussed in Session 1. Study them closely along with the associated Scriptures that support them. Is there one particular principle that you need to focus on and apply more readily in your life?

Personal Reflections:

What did I learn about God this week?

What did I learn about myself this week?

Journal Space

Chapter 2: Identity

What is identity? The dictionary might define personal identity as the characteristics that make people who they are, the things that separate them from the others around them. So, it is the way a person would answer the question: Who am I? While there are many commonalities among human beings, each person has an individual identity that helps to separate and distinguish one person from another. The more obvious physical components of identity have to do with hair, eyes, face shape, body type, gender, and others. Other parts of a person's identity are those that might not be so clear on the surface; they are the pieces that make up the personality, strengths, interests, aptitudes, and talents. These are harder to identify and can be difficult to pinpoint without some self-reflection and analysis.

But these components are only part of a much bigger picture. When considering the fuller scope of the concept, we look at who we are in God's eyes, as unique and specific creations of the Master Designer of the universe; we investigate how He has provided strengths and gifts that fit with His design and master plan for our lives; we consider the things that catch our interest and focus and learn about how we are "wired"; and we sometimes grapple with our own perception of ourselves as that compares to the views that other people seem to have of us. God created each person as a masterpiece, for the purpose of enjoying a personal relationship with Him and reflecting His glory to all those around.

> *We are unique and specific creations of the Master Designer.*

Personal identity, how we view ourselves, can be conceptualized in three domains, according to psychologist Carducci (2009). These domains are personal, social, and collective. The personal domain is where the focus is on the private self; where our own thoughts, ideas, goals, and emotions help us define who we are. Just as it might seem, the social domain is more dependent on interactions with others and the feedback we get from them about our popularity, reputation, and value. The collective domain allows for some definition of who we are based on belonging to a larger group or community. For example, ethnicity, occupation, or religious associations are part of the collective domain.

Each one of these domains plays a role in how we think of ourselves. Often, one of the domains will have a more dominant influence than the others based on the way each person is individually bent or inclined. Social media has become one of those powerful forces in society today, causing many to create a false identity based on how they want to be perceived. Comparing ourselves with others can also become a very dangerous thing in which to engage because of its potentially devastating effects.

There is a domain that transcends all of these and should truly be the most dominant influence: what God says about who we are. God's truths about who we are form the foundation of the development of our identities and should be a line of demarcation and separation from the rest of the world who do not know Christ. Those who have accepted the gift of salvation and walk in a personal relationship with God can know these truths and learn to understand who they are based on the truths of God's Word and His perspective, because in doing this we truly realize who we are because of Whose we are!

In modern day psychological principles, identity plays a key role in understanding of self. Erikson's theories about adolescent development focus on the formation of identity. Once the developmental pieces are in place for a person to be aware of others and their perspectives, and cognitive abilities are such that a person can process and reflect on their own awareness and sense of self, the beginnings of a certain level of identity begin to manifest themselves. Generally, by the time a person gets to the age of late adolescence or early adulthood, he or she is able to define and identify personal traits, interests, talents, strengths, characteristics, likes and dislikes, and so on.

> *The most dominant influence should be what God says about who we are!*

As noted earlier, each person is a treasured creation of God and His desire is to have a personal relationship with each one. For those who are in that relationship because we have accepted the gift of salvation through Christ, we are adopted to be God's children. That is who we are. As God's children, we are heirs to all of the spiritual blessings that God provides for us because He allows us to be part of His family. This identity and position in Him does not change based on our actions, performance, external appearance, or any other thing that another person may use to measure us or attempt to determine our worth. Our position in Him was not based on any of those things to start with, so there is no way they can affect who we are in Christ. Yet so many people today describe themselves and allow their self-image to be based on something they do or how well they think they have done it. We see here a contrast of identity based on the unchanging truth of God's Word that says we are dearly loved children of God (our position in Christ) and the values of the world and feedback of others that influence our own perspective of ourselves.

Let's look more closely at what God says about who we are.

Loved. One of the most well-known verses in the Bible, John 3:16, clearly states that God loved and still loves the world. The kind of love He displayed by sending His Son to the world was the greatest type of unselfish and generous love that could ever be shown. He did not discriminate in any way or offer the gift of His Son to just certain people. He said that whoever believed and accepted the gift could gain eternal life with Him. These truths are echoed in I John 4:9-10. These verses tell us that God initiated a relationship with us by loving us first and sending His Son to be the payment for our sins. His was the supreme example of sacrificial love in that He reached out to us and made the ultimate sacrifice for us!

If you have never received this gift, it is not too late to do so now. In His great love, He is reaching out His hand to offer you an eternal relationship with Him. It does not require you to DO anything, you must just simply believe that Jesus is the Son of God and He came to offer you the one and only way to have a relationship with God. You can simply speak to God right now and tell Him that you realize that without the gift of His Son you are lost on your own, that you accept His gift, and that you want to enter into a forever relationship with Him. If you're not quite sure how this all works, talk to a trusted friend who you know is already one of God's children, or a pastor of a Bible-based church.

The final verses of Romans 8 reinforce the message of the love of God for us and how powerful it is. Paul reminds us that there is nothing that can ever possibly come against us or cause us to be separated from His love. His love transcends any type of earthly trouble or trial we will ever face; it is stronger than death and life and all the evil forces; it conquers all things of the present and anything that is to come. There is literally nothing that can come between us and His love. The New Living Translation says it like this: "No power in the sky above or in the earth below—indeed, nothing in all creation will ever be able to separate us from the love of God that is revealed in Christ Jesus our Lord" (v. 39). That is a pretty intense and supernatural kind of love.

There are many, many verses in the Bible that communicate His incredible love that forms the basis for our identity in Him. Consider the precious story of the shepherd who left his flock to go in search of the one beloved lost sheep (Matthew 18, Luke 15). That is the kind of special and individualized love we have from our Good Shepherd! We have highlighted some characteristics of that love: unselfish, generous, sacrificial, and powerful. These should reinforce to us how much He loves us and the great lengths to which He has gone in order to communicate that love to us. We are truly His beloved children and along with that He has assigned great value to us and given us a special status.

Valued. Every part of creation is an aspect of God's handiwork, specially designed and intricately woven together. Psalm 19:1 says that "the heavens declare the glory of God and the firmament shows His handiwork." There is no doubt when you stop to take in the beauty and intricacy of the nature around you, it can easily boggle your mind to think of the masterful design and Creator behind all of it. Consider an artist, like Michelangelo for example. He created some exquisite masterpieces, took time planning and executing those plans, gave extreme attention to the minutest of details, and gave the world some of the most highly valued pieces of art in history which are still revered to this day. Now, imagine, if you will, the artist, God. He created the heavens and the earth, the stars and all the galaxies, the earth, sun, and moon, and all of the plants, animals, and fish. He creates each and every human being and each one is planned and designed down to the smallest atom. So intimately is He involved in every human being's life that no one is created except by Him, and each one has immeasurable value because of Who the Creator/Artist is. When God created the world, He also gave humans a special place and value above the rest of creation.

Not only are humans considered by God to be masterpieces of incredible worth in the middle of the rest of His masterful tapestry of handiwork, humans were given a status that is beyond that of any other created thing. He made us in His image according to Genesis 1:26-27. Though it is not a physical image that we share since God is a spiritual being, we are like Him in that we have special intellectual and spiritual abilities, we are relational beings such that we need to have a relationship with God and others, and we were given the responsibility of being caretakers of the rest of creation. The value we have as beings created in His image is incredibly important in how we see ourselves and the purpose He has given to each person to be His representatives here on earth.

Unique. We can easily see by looking around us on any given day that God's creation includes more variety than we can even comprehend. From beetles to snowflakes to the colors in nature, it can confound us to try to take in the many distinctions God has used in creating the world around us. This concept applies just as readily to each human being created. Each one is unique, individual, and distinct from the next. There is no other you! You are tailor made…one of a kind…a masterpiece! This makes you special, and it also means that because of your uniqueness and the distinctive characteristics with which God designed you, you have a special purpose. Psalm 139 talks about the personal care and attention God gives as He "knits" together each one of us in the womb. He is intimately involved in making and designing each person; nothing and no one is by accident. Each person is planned and designed long before birth, with a purposeful intention. Don't let that go to waste; embrace your unique qualities, strengths, personality, and upbringing because God wants to use you!

Though these are all quite abstract concepts, it is important to be able to not only understand them in an intellectual way, but to internalize them so they become known, accepted, and embraced at the heart-level. If we only acknowledge them at the head-level, they do not have an opportunity to be personalized and incorporated into who we are, which is the only way they can truly shape us and how we live. Meditation on the Scriptures can help us understand them at the heart-level and then we can make applications of these truths into our lives as they affect the way we see ourselves and then how we act on those beliefs.

Loved. Valued. Unique.

As we begin the process of understanding our own identity, how God has made and designed us, what experiences He has allowed to shape us, and how He brings together those things that make us who we are today, we also know that He uses all of those pieces to give us a place in His work in the world. He calls us, equips us, enables us, and gives us the privilege of being part of His Kingdom ministries on earth. (One translation of Ephesians 2: 10 says: "God has made us what we are. In Christ Jesus, God made us to do good works, which God planned in advance for us to live our lives doing.") Through this increased understanding and because of it, we can sense the purpose He gives us and as we discover how He has wired us, we can begin to align our life choices accordingly. But this increased understanding is a process, a process of discovery that never really ends in our lifetime. The goal here is to begin to identify some of these components, bring further clarity and definition to things that you may have noticed but have not fully explored or recognized about yourself, and give you some foundational pieces upon which to build the concepts that will help you as you move forward in a lifelong journey.

Even before we can truly understand our life's purpose and mission, we must seek to comprehend who He created us to be. Many times, frustration comes if we try to find our purpose in life before we determine who we are (Costa, 2016). People often try to jump into life before they have quite figured out who they are and what God has called them to do. It can be the cause of great confusion and ultimately disillusionment.

This journey of discovery will encompass self-analysis, assessments, discussions and a few other tools to bring to light strengths and abilities, personality traits, passions and values, and also life experiences thus far. Strengths and abilities are things that come naturally, the talents God has wired within us as well as those things that are skills which have been honed. Personality is word we use to describe the inner components of a person that affect and influence the way each one thinks, feels, and behaves. Passions and values are the intangibles that drive us, excite us, and are reflected in what we care deeply about, what moves us, and what we are not willing to compromise. Then finally, experience comprises all of the events, circumstances, and situations in life that God orchestrates (though some of these happen because He allows them rather than causes them) in order to bring about the good things He has for us and for His Kingdom purposes (Rom. 8:28).

Discussion:

Why is understanding identity important in better understanding and clarifying life purpose/mission?

Are there *other* components to identity that you believe are important to a better understanding of who you are?

Assignments:

Meditation 1

1) Read Ephesians 3:17-19 and describe what those verses tell you about God's love. What characteristics are evident there?
2) Read I John 3:1 and think about what it means to you. Again, look for the characteristics of God's love.
3) Using a concordance or a key word search tool, find 3 more verses that express God's love for you and then consider how all of these verses contribute to your greater understanding and acceptance of how much God loves you and how that affects how you see yourself.

Meditation 2

1) Read through Psalm 139 in its entirety once or twice. What are some key themes you notice?

2) Read through verses 13-18 a couple of times. Summarize them briefly and then identify what you think these verses mean.

How does this apply to you?

When you think about the value you have in God's eyes, the care He took in designing you, the detailed knowledge He has about every part of you, how do you feel? What does it say about who you are?

Given these truths from God's Word, what does that change for you (beliefs, thinking, actions…)?

Personal Reflections:

What did I learn about God this week?

What did I learn about myself this week?

A Young Adult's Guide

Journal Space

Chapter 3: Strengths and Abilities

Strength is a word that denotes power, courage, tenacity, and potency. In a context such as we are using here, it conveys the ability to repeatedly do something well. Many times, strengths and abilities are things that come very naturally and easily for a person, such as an innate talent, but sometimes they are built and developed out of a lot of effort or hard work, such as a learned skill. For example, there are athletes who show early physical abilities and tendencies toward kinesthetic coordination. They may go on to be professional athletes and enjoy physical activities for years. Others may not be born with any great and obvious natural proficiency, but through a lot of hard work and determination, they may be able to compete at elite levels also. So, whether a person has early inclinations toward a certain talent or those strengths become more evident based on effort or experience, they are often seen by others as something a person does well…something notable that stands out in a positive way. Remember, God gives each of us strengths. Yours are not the same as your brother's or sister's or best friend's; this is not a comparison or competition.

God gives each person a group of gifts. This unique combination of physical skills, intellectual abilities, emotions, thoughts, and approaches work together to be the basis of what is needed to carry out what God calls us to do in the world. They are part of the equipment and implements He provides for us. That is why it is so important to recognize them and be willing to submit them for His use and glory. There will be times when these strengths and abilities are used in a variety of roles, sometimes as a leader, other times as a supporting member, and still other times when you are not even quite certain of your role, but you know that somehow God is working through you to accomplish His greater plan. Remember that the most important factor is to be the best you God created you to be, not comparing yourself with others or vying for a different set of gifts. Every person, and the role God designates, is important because the gifts and calling are from God.

Be the best you God created you to be.

It can be quite a challenge to sit and think of what your gifts and strengths might be. We are taught from a young age not to brag or be egocentric, so we often neglect to consider these things. Sometimes we also struggle with self-esteem issues where we focus too much on our perceived shortcomings rather than identifying and developing our strengths. So, it's okay to take some time to think about this and truly seek to pinpoint your characteristics and talents. As you consider what your abilities, strengths, and talents might be, reflect on what you feel confident in doing, what others have said in the past about what seems to come naturally for you, what you enjoy doing and have a sense of doing well. Think about specific accomplishments, events, or actions where you could sense that you were operating from a position of strength. If you are struggling with this, do not be afraid to ask a trusted family member of friend to help you think this through and provide some helpful feedback.

There is a well-known tool that has been used for the last 15 years or so which is built on the concept that we can accomplish much more in life if we operate based on an informed sense of our strengths. Whereas some people spend a lot of time trying to focus on overcoming areas of weakness or setting goals in order to achieve something new that will bring about greater strength, the theory here is that people are better at what they are doing when they are living out of their strengths. You can read more about this and take the assessment at the Strengths Finder website (http://www.strengthstest.com/strengths-finder-themes).

Discussion:

What are some of the strengths and abilities you feel confident about? Are there some that you are more tentative about? Try to keep this separate from your personality, as that will be addressed in the next section.

Are there any areas where you have developed a skill, but you don't necessarily feel it is a strength because it not very natural to you and it often feels like a chore or a drain?

What are some areas you are interested in but have never had a chance to "test out" to see if you might have some natural ability?

Assignments:

Meditation

Read Exodus 36:1 & 2, I Chronicles 15:22, and II Chronicles 2:14.

How do these verses relate to the topic of strengths and abilities? How does this help your understanding and application?

Assessment

Take the Strengths Finder assessment online at www.strengthstest.com (there is a cost involved) and print out your results.

-OR-

Use the list of themes/strengths found at https://www.strengthsquest.com/192458/clifton-strengths-theme-quick-reference-card.aspx to select what you believe to be your strengths. Narrow your list to the top five.

Consider the top five strengths discovered in the assessment tool you used and then provide examples of how you have seen some of them to be true in your daily life.

Personal Reflections:

What did I learn about God this week?

What did I learn about myself this week?

Journal Space

Chapter 4: Personality

Much has been said and written about personality theories in the field of Psychology. You could read about this topic for hours or even days, but most people probably have a conceptualization of what personality is because it is a commonplace topic. Why is it important? Why do we study it? How can it help us? The study of personality can stem from a desire to understand our own feelings and behavior choices better. We may also seek to understand if there are changes we can make so as to retrain ourselves in certain areas for growth and improvement. It can be beneficial also when we are able to understand others better as this may help us in our interactions and relationships with them. Ryckman (2013) states: "We can establish and clarify the goals that serve to motivate and focus our efforts, thereby enabling us to experience personal growth within the context of making contributions to society (p. 3)."

Personality theorists have taken a variety of approaches in understanding the way people behave. Some theorists have looked only at external behaviors to make their observations while others considered the unobservable forces that contribute to behaviors and aspects of personality. There is no single theory that can be said for certain is the best or most complete. But the four criteria that most theorists seek to satisfy in their research are the ability to describe, explain, predict, and control variables with the intention of providing explanations for how and why people behave in the ways they do. Many of the theoretical explanations found in Personality Psychology include concepts such as temperament, constructs, traits, and types. These are ways of organizing and categorizing ideas and observations for use in assessments and applications.

> *Personality influences how we think, feel, and behave.*

For the sake of simplification and our purposes here, we can settle on the concept that personality is the internal force (though also affected by external factors) that influences and affects how we think, feel, and behave. When we study a personality type, we are able to see some dominant characteristics that come from a person's genetic background as well as from environmental influences. For example, if we say that a person is outgoing or extroverted, that is a natural part of the way that person thinks, feels, and acts such that he or she enjoys being around people, is not shy, and thrives in social settings and through interactions with others. So that personality characteristic, extraversion, influences the person's thoughts and feelings, and affects decisions that are made by that person. Each person has a unique way of interacting and responding to any given set of physical, social, and cultural settings, stimuli, and situations. We often use descriptors, such as extrovert, to help us understand and frame the way people behave and in doing so, we can then figure out how to relate to them or what to expect of them. We do this about ourselves as well, and many times we do it without even realizing it. And yet, these personality traits can be a bit hard to pin down or capture, so it may be helpful to participate in an actual personality assessment.

As far as personality assessments, there are many and they reflect the theoretical basis upon which they were created. The majority of those would be administered in session with a psychologist or therapist. There are also numerous tests available online that claim to provide feedback, though many of them are not tested for validity or reliability. They can be fun and funny, but are probably not worth too much time or attention. There are, however, some great ones that have been tested and tried which may be able to provide some valuable insights for you as you seek to further your understanding of yourself. Several assessments will be part of the Assignments for this chapter.

Discussion:

What are some of the personality traits you possess and how do you feel about them?

How will knowing more about your personality be helpful in pursuing the dreams you have and the calling God has given you?

What do you think may be some potential pitfalls when we consider this topic?

Assignments:

Meditation

Read I Corinthians 12:27 and Romans 12:4. These verses talk about how we are all different, but unique and part of the body of Christ. How does this relate to the topic of personality?

Read Luke 10:38-42 in which the sisters Mary and Martha opened their home to Jesus. How does this passage contribute to your understanding of personality?

Provide an example from the Bible where you think a person's personality either contributed well to their work for the Lord or detracted from it and explain your ideas about this.

Assessments

Take the following three free online assessments listed below and print/document the results so you can see a spectrum of personality traits.

Free online Type Indicator – (in the form of MBTI) = 16personalities.com

Free online DiSC assessment = www.123tes.com/disc-personality-test

Smalley's animal types = https://www.quotev.com/quiz/5946131/Lion-beaver-Otter-and-Golden-Retriever-Test

Based on the personality assessments, what do you believe are some of the strengths and weaknesses (areas for growth) within your personality?

How do you find the balance between accepting and embracing who you are and how God has made you, but also addressing those areas of your personality that need work and greater submission to the Holy Spirit?

Personal Reflections:

What did I learn about God this week?

What did I learn about myself this week?

Journal Space

Chapter 5: Passions and Values

A person's heart and desires are those things that are very important to him or her; we may even be able to refer to them as passions. For some people, these are easy to pinpoint, for others, they take a bit of digging or may require more life experiences for them to surface. In either case, it is what excites and motivates a person, it comes from an inner desire or strong feeling about something, it generally requires some action which then leads to great fulfillment. Values are what we consider to have worth, importance, and significance; when we value something (or someone) we hold it in high regard, guard it, and even treasure it. Matthew 6:21 says that where our treasure is, our heart will also be. So, our passions and values are linked at the heart level; they come from the core of our being.

Then, of course, it is best when our passions align with bringing about God's Kingdom plan on earth and have eternally significant results. When our heart and passions are focused on things that are for our own gain or fulfillment without regard for what God desires, then we are no different from those who do not follow Christ. While we may have some success in that way, it is limited in that it does not further God's work in the world and provides only temporary outcomes and partial fulfillment.

Generally, by the time of emerging adulthood, we have a couple of ideas of what our heart is urging us to, what excites our passions. Let's take a look at the life of Betty Greene (Benge & Benge, 1999). Early in her life, she developed a fascination for aviation and loved the adventures of Amelia Earhart and Charles Lindbergh. As a young girl, she had the opportunity to see Lindbergh in person after his flight across the Atlantic and from that early age, she knew she wanted to be a pilot. In World War II, she flew military planes with the Women Airforce Service Pilots (WASPs) and once the War was over she continued on in aviation. Her strong desire to be a pilot and her love for God motivated her to work with several others to establish Mission Aviation Fellowship in 1945, an agency that still continues to share the love of Jesus to isolated people using aviation and now technology (www.maf.org). Betty Greene is a great example of someone who found her passions early and she ended up living a life where she used her passions to further the Kingdom of God.

Values are also important here. If our behaviors match our values, we have a sense of harmony and contentment; but if there is something out of alignment in this area, that can contribute to an inner feeling of unrest, unhappiness, a lack of fulfillment, or of something just being wrong. As we identify and acknowledge our values, then they can inform life's decisions and keep us focused on pursuing what is of utmost importance to us.

Passions and values come from the core of our being.

There are some values that are and should be firm, lasting, and fixed. These are the foundational, bedrock kinds of values; the ones that house our core beliefs and deep spiritual convictions. Some of these may include: worship only God and have no other gods before Him, love others as you would yourself, live a moral and godly life, avoid hypocrisy, steward what you have been given, and forgive others quickly. Jesus spent a lot of time explaining how the values of the Kingdom of God are quite opposite to the values of the world and even of the religious leaders of that time. The importance of these cannot be overstated and the pursuit of them is a lifelong endeavor. There are also other values that are conceptualized more like characteristics or traits. Some of them may be based on our underlying spiritual value system, but others are simply personal preferences and may change or shift with time.

When we think about what we value, we can be very broad or very specific. As we focus in on understanding our own individual set of values, there are some tools we can use that will help us narrow in on some of those themes that will help guide our thoughts as we later consider life purpose ideas. Sometimes values are so much a part of us that we take them for granted and forget they are there. For example, some people are very strongly connected to both their immediate family as well as extended family, so much so that they would not consider living in a different town from their family members. If given an opportunity to take a job in a different state, that family value and priority would be a guiding factor in the decision. While they realize that family is important to them, they may have never really understood how strongly that value influences their life decisions and priorities. In some cases, people struggle with some dissonance in life and may not be able to identify which value(s) may be compromised such that they have an inner feeling of discomfort of discontent.

Perhaps a person starts out in a career in banking because it is a family expectation and it has worked well as a vocation for that family for several generations. Soon, however, that young person is bored, unsatisfied, and disinterested. It would be important then to get back to the basics and begin to identify what values and ideals are not matching up with real life. Is there a value for altruism and philanthropy that is being ignored? Is self-expression and creativity not being cultivated? Or perhaps there is a shift in priorities that comes about which needs to be acknowledged and applied. In either case, values can be very powerful influences for guiding life choices and pursuits. Having a sense of self-awareness in this area will be significant in contributing to the whole picture of life purpose and mission.

To help identify and define your passions and values, take some time to go through these exercises.

1) Think about a time when you feel you were truly happy, content, and fulfilled.
    a) What was the situation? What were you doing that brought about this sense of happiness and contentment?
    b) What factors seemed to contribute to this?
    c) Were there people involved and what might they have contributed?
2) Think about a time when you felt most proud or accomplished.
    a) What was the situation? What did you do that brought about this sense of pride and accomplishment?

b) What factors seemed to contribute to this?
c) Were there people involved and what might they have contributed?

Discussion:

Based on the exercises you just completed, what are some things about which you feel passionate? What excites you about them?

What are the 5 most important things/ideas/traits to you? Why?

Assignments:

Meditation

Read Matthew 6:19-21; 33. How do these verses speak to you in terms of what you value?

Read Psalm 1:1-3. These verses talk about delighting in the Law of the Lord. How does this speak to your heart and how are these verses related to the topic of passions and values?

Assessments

Use the List of Common Values on the following page to help you determine yours. Find those that resonate the most deeply with you and circle them. From there, list out your top ten in no particular order, and then prioritize the list to your best ability. You can do this by starting at the bottom of the list and comparing the 2 values listed there and moving up the one that outranks the other. You can work through the list several times in this way in order to get the list into the correct order. Remember this is your list, so if you think of other values that were not on the list that you would like to add in, you can also do that.

List of Common Values

Circle or mark the words that resonate the most deeply with you, at the level of a 9 or 10 (out of 10). Notice that some of them naturally go together and can be combined.

Accountability	Dependability	Openness
Accuracy	Determination	Optimism
Achievement	Diversity	Order
Altruism	Effectiveness	Peace
Ambition	Efficiency	Perfection
Assertiveness	Empathy	Popularity
Authenticity	Equality	Practicality
Autonomy	Excellence	Reliability
Balance	Expertise	Resourcefulness
Beauty	Faith	Results
Being the best	Family	Self-control
Belonging	Fidelity	Service
Boldness	Fitness	Spirituality
Calmness	Generosity	Spontaneity
Carefulness	Growth	Stability
Challenge	Happiness	Strength
Cheerfulness	Hard Work	Structure
Clear-mindedness	Health	Success
Commitment	Honor	Team-work
Community	Humor	Thoughtfulness
Compassion	Insightfulness	Timeliness
Competitiveness	Intelligence	Tradition
Consistency	Joy	Trustworthiness
Continuous Improvement	Justice	Uniqueness
Contribution	Kindness	Unity
Cooperation	Leadership	Vision
Creativity	Learning	Wealth
Decisiveness	Love	Wisdom
	Loyalty	

Another exercise you can do is take the List of Life Categories below and write a value statement or two for each one (Stoltzfus, 2009). Note, as you go through it, which categories seem more important to you than the others. If you are having difficulty pinpointing things here, think about how an impartial observer of your life would comment about you based on how you spend your time and energies. Then also consider which areas you would like to pursue more strongly as you mature and move forward in life.

1. Faith
2. Family
3. Career/Vocation
4. Money
5. Health and recreation
6. Community
7. Living environment
8. Personal growth

Personal Reflections:

What did I learn about God this week?

What did I learn about myself this week?

Journal Space

Chapter 6: Experience

It does not take much to describe what we mean by experience, so let's take a look instead at what the benefits of experience can be in the context of our discussion. There are many life events and circumstances that contribute to how we perceive ourselves and the world around us. As we consider the previous topics, one of the main ways that we are able to identify these other components come about because of our experiences. The opportunities we have to engage in activities, service of others, learning, and a variety of social circumstances, the more we are able to discern about ourselves. Things we have gone through in life, even when they are because of trial or hardship, bring perspective and help shape us.

A personal example here is from my college years. I first began by pursuing a major in Nursing. I had always had an interest in the field of medicine, loved to study Science in my K-12 years, and I had grown up in an overseas setting where medical vocations and services were very helpful. It seemed a natural fit for me, and yet at the end of my first year I was frustrated, hated my lab classes, and was doubting my abilities to complete the degree (and certainly did not feel that I would enjoy any of it). What I learned about myself in that situation was that I am not very coordinated and kinesthetic such that even the hands-on requirements of the labs were taxing and stressful for me. You could ask me to sit down and write a paper or explain a topic to someone else, and that was easy and enjoyable to me. I loved opportunities I had to learn new things and in doing so, I would try to break them into concepts that I could explain to someone else. So, after my freshman year, I changed my major and went on to pursue Psychology and Education. Because of the exposure to a variety of settings that I had not truly experienced before, I was able to sort out what some of my abilities were (and weren't) and take time to evaluate what was fulfilling for me and where I could see God using me effectively. I was able to make the most of challenging circumstances and draw from my experiences to better hone in on the practical ways I could live out the calling I felt to help people.

Things we have gone through help shape us.

There are also many other cases where young adults really need to get out and experience more things, more of what life has to offer in order to begin to pinpoint what makes you tick, what engages you, where you feel like you can make a contribution, what seems to click internally and provide a sense of that sweet spot of natural flow. This does not mean that you only do things you like to do or feel comfortable in. It is also important to challenge yourself by doing things you might not enjoy at first, or by doing things that seem to be greater than your own abilities. These are also very valuable experiences because through them you learn more about yourself. You often gain the most insights when things are tough, maybe even when you fail at something, and come to the end of your own ideas about yourself. While it will likely be more difficult to revisit the painful memories and experiences, the value in it will outweigh any struggle you might have. It is beneficial to take the time to evaluate and examine your life experiences, be willing to learn new things about yourself, and maybe even take a step back and rethink things based on what circumstances or situations have brought to light.

Do some "business" with God!

Purposeful Living

As you examine life-changing events, both good and bad, you need to determine how they shaped you, how you were affected in the long-term. But then you also need to see how God used them in your life. If you did not allow Him space to work in a particular instance, it's not too late to still learn something, but you may need to take some time and do some "business" with God.

Discussion:

As you consider your life this far, there may be life experiences you already know God is using to help define you and guide your future. Share one of those and how you can see God's hand at work.

Are there some experiences you are still waiting on God to bring revelation as to His purpose or plan in them? Share one of those and the questions you still have.

Assignments:

Meditation:

David's life gives us a good example of how God used his experience with a slingshot to prepare him for a big task. Read I Samuel 17:31-54 (or the whole chapter in order to get the full context). Explain how God prepared David for this challenge.

Exercise:

Write a biographical sketch focusing on what you define as life-shaping events in your life. Delineate what those events were, how they shaped you, and how you see God's hand in them. Then focus on what heart message (what you learned at your heart/soul level) you took away and how that message might help others.

Personal Reflections:

What did I learn about God this week?

What did I learn about myself this week?

Journal Space

Chapter 7: Calling

One of the key areas we as humans find ourselves trying to identify and define for ourselves is our reason for being and our specific place in this world. We look for understanding as to why we are here on the earth, why we were made the way we are, what we should be doing with our lives, what we can be doing to live a life of meaning and value, how our lives matter. These are no small questions and they are not answered in one quick moment. The answers we embrace, though, are often what we conceptualize as our calling in life, so they are worth the time and potential labor they may require.

As Christians, we are all called. We are called to live out our core beliefs and values in this world, in our everyday lives. We are called to be engaged in the society around us reflecting the power, grace, love, peace, hope, and light that we have from our Father. We are called to live out the directives to love God with all our beings and to love our neighbors as ourselves. In addition, we know that we need to go and make disciples, inviting others into a relationship with God and encouraging them in their walk with Him. These are the things God has called us to do as part of the responsibilities He gives us when we become His followers. So then, any specific calling we have will include the elements of these callings we have as Christ followers. In other words, our broader Christian calling will be the lens and filter through which we also see, understand, and apply our own specific and personal calling.

In this process, we must first believe wholeheartedly that God has a great plan for us. Each person must believe and accept this to be true about him or herself. God has work for us to do in this world; He wants us join in on what He is doing to help further His Kingdom. In order to do this, we will need to participate, engage, and be purposeful about using the gifts He has given us, and in very practical ways be His hand and feet, His representatives in this world!

As Christians, we are all called.

There are many examples in the Bible of how God called people. Story after story shows how God called people and used them to accomplish His Story. You can look at the lives of Moses, Noah, Job, Abraham, Joseph, Samuel, Ruth, David, Esther, Mary, Paul, Peter, etc… and each of them has a story of calling. Notice that He only used those who are willing and obedient; this is particularly evident in Jonah's calling. This means He does not remove the element of human choice; He does not impose His will on anyone. Therefore, even before a calling is given, it is important to cultivate a heart of willingness and eager obedience. He also does not set aside a person's desires, talents, passions, personality, or even opinions. Since He created each one of us, He knows those details and He uses the things He has given us for His glory. He does not force anyone, what He does instead is say, like He did to His disciples on earth, "Come with me, follow me, abide with me." His calling is liberating and exciting; He brings out the best in us as He leads and guides us to do and become what He knows we can do and become because of our relationship with Him and through His grace and power.

Peter's life provides a great example for us. As Jesus called him, He offered a new focus and purpose in life: to go from being a fisherman to being a fisher of men (an analogy Peter could relate to, so we see that Jesus already knew him well). Jesus saw in him far more than Peter would have believed at the time of his calling. After Jesus called him, He even gave him a new name – though he had been called Simon, Jesus said he would now also be known as Cephas (Peter), which means Rock (John 1:42). Peter later played a key role in the foundation of the

> *You can always continue forward in living a purposeful life.*

early Church. Jesus saw his potential and drew him to come alongside, join Him in what He was doing in His ministry on earth, and begin to see the great contributions he could bring. Jesus knew him, loved him, and drew him to Himself. In that relationship, He called him and spoke into his soul.

Though we see that Peter became a fisher of men, we also need to understand that a calling is not exclusively tied to a job or vocation. Peter did become a leader in the church, though there may still have been times when he needed to support himself and his family by fishing, just as Paul supported his work by making tents. The key to understanding calling is to realize that it is pervasive, including our other pursuits in life and priorities. Family lives, social lives, hobbies and interests, and essentially our whole lives are to be lived in submission and obedience to the Holy Spirit's call (both in the general calling as Christ followers and in the specific sense of the calling He gives individually). Just as we do not separate out some part of our lives as lived for ourselves and some lived for God's glory, we also need to adopt a mindset that realizes the application of our calling and ultimately our mission in life is reasonably applied to all areas of life (Rom. 12: 1-2).

In his book providing biblical models and tools for the discovery of life purpose, Stolzfus (2009) offers a list of possible ways that you may come to understand your calling. The following is adapted from his original list.

1) God reveals it directly to you.

2) God arranges circumstances to bring your calling to light in a "destiny" sort of way.

3) God uses Scripture to reveal a calling.

4) God provides someone to name or confirm your calling.

5) You are drawn to a need. You feel called to serve others who have that specific need.

6) You experience suffering such that you want to help others based on those experiences.

7) You experience some success which reveals to you how you can use that on behalf of others

8) You have an early and extreme gifting/ability.

9) You have an early dream (maybe even as a child) that reveals a specific calling.

10) You experience a strong righteous discontent that awakens a call toward a cause.

11) You have a community or familial call. Based on the upbringing in your family or community, you embrace the collective purpose.

12) God uses time, events, circumstances, and insights to progressively reveal your calling.

In some cases, like #12 states, you may not be able to identify your calling immediately or in a brief period of time. You may need to devote some serious time and energy into seeking the Lord and asking Him for help in understanding and wisdom. Be patient; He will show you what He wants you to do in His timing. Perhaps as you continue through this process of outlining your life purpose, you will also come to a greater understanding of what God is calling you to do. In the meantime, you can work on building your relationship with Him and serving Him as you obey His general calling. Remember, you can always continue forward in living a purposeful life by daily obeying the two commandments to love God first and above all else, and love others.

Discussion:

Do you need to have a specific calling in order to have a purposeful life? What happens if you are not able to articulate a personal calling in your life?

Assignments:

Meditation:

Read Romans 12:1-2. The end of the first verse presents the idea of worshipping God and serving Him. What does the verse say is required for this type of worship and what is the motivation also noted in the verse? How will a renewed mind help you as you seek to determine His calling?

Exercise:

Talk to someone you know who lives life with a definite and focused purpose/mission. Talk to him or her about calling and how God showed him/her how to live with purpose for His glory. What are some things you can learn and apply from this conversation?

Personal Reflections:

What did I learn about God this week?

What did I learn about myself this week?

Journal Space

Chapter 8: Life Purpose/Mission

Now, at this point in our process, we gather all that we have learned about ourselves and use those discoveries as the basis for defining our purpose or mission in life. Some refer to it as a credo, a mantra, a philosophy, or even a personal constitution. As noted in the beginning of this journey, we can compare our lives in this way to a business with an articulated mission, vision, and set of values. Similarly, in our lives, if we wish to move forward with intentional living and purpose, we must set those ideas in place in our lives in order to have them as guiding parameters. This allows then for all choices and decisions we have to make to be evaluated next to our defined purpose or mission statement. (These two terms, purpose and mission, can be used synonymously.) The list of specific values delineated earlier, along with those found in God's Word can give discernment in ethically challenging situations and provide support for the underlying purpose statement. When faced with potentially life-changing options, the statement can be a filter to sort out what will increase and what will diminish the opportunities to stay right in the middle of what you believe God has purposed for you.

It is worth noting that whenever we are not intentional about the choices we make or try to live life without the guiding principles of the purpose statement, we end up living life by default. This is what happens when people float through life or bounce around based on circumstances. In addition, other people's expectations and demands can easily become the leading influence for life's decisions. This leads quickly to frustration, disappointment, and disillusionment, not to mention that we are disconnected from what God designed for us to do.

God will reveal His ways and timing.

The culminating exercise then, is to be able to gather together the thoughts, ideas, feelings, observations, etc. that you have gleaned throughout this process and put them into a sentence or two that will become a life purpose/mission statement. This is not something that will be done in one sitting. Rather it is a process and may require reworking and revising so that it resonates clearly as a statement to live by. Throughout your life you will need to keep this present and be willing to revisit it to make adjustments or changes during various seasons of life. You may also come up with a statement, live with it for a while, and then feel the need to make some modifications as the Holy Spirit gives you more insights. Do not be afraid of this process. There is not one, exactly perfect way of expressing these ideas with words, so we do the best we can with words to convey the concepts that come from deep within. God will unfold and reveal things according to His ways and timing.

In order to begin, you will need to review each of the discussions, exercises, and your personal notes from the things you have learned. You can then make yourself some lists of highlights or summaries that will provide the basis for the formation of your life purpose/mission statement. Look for themes; consider the way the Holy Spirit has brought out certain things and how He has been tugging at your heart.

Following are some exercises to help in composing your life purpose/mission statement. Try several ways of expressing these ideas and remember, there is no perfect version. The goal is to provide yourself with a guiding statement that is specific enough to be helpful, but not so hard to remember that you can never really own it. This may take some time and will require careful reflection, so be patient with yourself in this process. It may also be worthwhile to glance through some sample statements that other people have written, which can be done quite easily by searching for them online. You can use them to trigger your own ideas and inspirations, but ultimately, your statement will be your own and will uniquely reflect God's design and imprint on your life.

Assignment:

Exercise:

Method 1

1) WHAT?

   What do you believe God would like to communicate through your life?
   - What themes seem to be surfacing that you get excited and passionate about and that you really feel God would like to speak through you to others?
   - What are you most excited to do with your life?
   - Are there any areas of specific impact?
   - Are there certain life situations that have ignited your passion?

   Example: I want to share God's love and acceptance in both word and deed...

2) WHO?

   Is there a specific group or type of people you would like to impact with your life?
   - Are there specific people (age, gender, culture, special needs) you are drawn to?

   Example: ...with those who struggle with issues related to self-esteem...

3) WHY?

    What is the desired outcome?
    - How will your efforts affect change?
    - What do you ultimately want to accomplish?
    - How will you benefit others?

    Example: …in order to build them up in Christ and help them engage in a true life-changing relationship with Him…

4) HOW?

    What is the channel for your message?
    - Is there a specific role, task, or project you sense God is calling you to?
    - Is there a more general application for your service?

    Example: …through my role as a teacher/mentor.

Sample Statement

"I want to share God's love and acceptance in both word and deed with those who struggle with issues related to self-esteem in order to build them up in Christ and help them engage in a true life-changing relationship with Him through my role as a teacher/mentor."

Method 2

Based on the self-discovery exercises you have completed and the insights you now have about who you are, spend some time working through the questions that follow.

1) What are you most passionate about pursuing? What is so important to you that you want to make a significant impact by pursuing that cause/issue? What do believe so strongly that you are willing to make it a high priority for your life?

2) What gifts, abilities, experiences, personality, and motivations do you bring that will help you in these pursuits? How has God equipped you to serve Him and contribute to His work in the world?

3) If there were no chance for failure, no limitations or obstacles, and any resources you might need are available, how would you want to live your life in order to make a difference in the world? What do you want to be known for in your lifetime?

Now, using these pieces, craft a statement that completes this beginning: "My mission in life is _____."

Make sure it is concise, but inclusive so that you feel it truly represents you, your values, and what you feel God is calling you to do.

Sample Statement

"My mission I life is to help bring healing to broken families by sharing my experiences and compassion with them. I want to be a beacon of hope to those who need it so they can know their value on God's eyes."

Personal Reflections:

What did I learn about God this week?

What did I learn about myself this week?

A Young Adult's Guide

Journal Space

Chapter 9: Conclusion

Through all of the exercises and discussions, reflections and Scriptures in this personal study, you have had an opportunity to make some great discoveries about yourself, about God, and about your relationship with God. He has created you uniquely, loves you extravagantly and personally, and invites you to engage with Him in bringing about His plans in the world. He did not just make you so that you can be happy in your own personal life, find fulfillment and pleasure, and settle in for a great time. His agenda is much bigger that that! He wants you to spread the love He gives you to others, He wants you to use the unique gifts, experiences, personality, passions, and calling to affect the world around you in ways that bring glory to Him and further His Kingdom!

The ultimate intention of this study has been to engage you in some thoughts that have culminated in the articulation a life mission statement. As you settle in to the expression of those concepts which accurately reflects your heart and passions, it will be wise and beneficial to write it down in a place that you will see fairly regularly. Look at it often so that it soaks into your soul and begins to take root there. If that fit does not seem to come about, go back to the exercises of Chapter 8 and work through them again. Do not be afraid of the time and effort it may take to create a statement that fits and feels right; it should be something that resonates with you, excites you, and motivates you each time you see it.

> *It should be something that resonates with you, excites you, and motivates you!*

As was mentioned several times previously, we have likened this to a strategic process that businesses go through to hone in on why they exist. Along with a mission statement, they often also have a set of several value statements to help members and stakeholders know what underlies the core of the mission. You may also find it helpful to write down a few value statements. They might be action statements that directly reflect your core beliefs. Following are some examples.

Love God first and above all else.

Treat others with kindness and respect.

Pursue growth and learning.

Forgive easily.

Be positive and hopeful.

As you continue to pursue clarity on your mission and values, remember that through the seasons of life, as you grow and change, your mission may adjust slightly in focus or application. There may be times of great activity and other situations where you feel as if you are still or even idle. They all have a purpose and God can use all of them for His glory, as long as you choose to live in submission to Him and walk in obedience. Don't be discouraged in times of confusion or adversity; instead remember that you have the Holy Spirit to help and guide you, and trust in God's goodness and faithfulness! But no matter what the time or season, the underlying, non-negotiable calling and expectation of all followers of Christ is to love God first and above all else, and to love others. Even if you feel as if you lose your way in terms of your personal mission and purpose, you can always get back to the unchanging truth of those fixed mandates.

In conclusion, never lose sight of the fact that God has a special purpose for you! You are part of His plan and you have something special to offer that nobody else can duplicate. There is nothing average or ordinary about you; you have been designed and created by the God of the universe and He wants you to represent Him to the world! So, embrace His love, His truth, and the blessings He gives you every day. Walk in the solid confidence that He has personally selected you to fulfill a great destiny!

References

Benge, J., & Benge, G. (1999). *Betty Greene: Wings to serve.* Seattle, WA: YWAM Publishing.

Carducci, B. J. (2009). *The psychology of personality: Viewpoints, research, and applications.* (2nd ed.). West Sussex, UK: Wiley-Blackwell.

Costa, K. (2016). *Know your why: Finding and fulfilling your calling in life.* Nashville, TN: W Publishing.

Keller, W. P. (1970). *A shepherd looks at Psalm 23.* Grand Rapids, MI: Zondervan.

Roberts, R. C. (2007). *Spiritual emotions: A psychology of Christian values.* Grand Rapids, MI: Eerdmans.

Ryckman, R. M. (2013). *Theories of personality* (10th ed.). Belmont, CA: Wadsworth.

Stanley, C.G. (2008). *God has a plan for your life: The discovery that makes all the difference.* Nashville, TN: Thomas Nelson.

Stoltzfus, T. (2009). *Christian life coaching handbook: Calling and destiny discovery tools for Christian life coaching.* Virginia Beach, VA: Coach22.Glossary

www.ingramcontent.com/pod-product-compliance
Lightning Source LLC
Chambersburg PA
CBHW071729040426
42446CB00011B/2274